GW00501915

I Married
into
Leprosy

Marion Cochrane MBE

Foreword

Marion's story was written by her with much encouragement from many who knew her. She had just completed her book about her father-in-law, Robert Cochrane, *The Edge of the Cliff*, and everyone said, "How about writing your story, Marion?"

As you'll see from this book, she had many unusual stories to tell.

The only condition she put on writing her stories was that someone else would have to put them together in a book! This is what her son Murray and daughter Hazel have now done.

We are very proud of Marion's life of dedication to people with leprosy – among the poorest and most marginalised people on earth - and for her amazing achievements together with our father Ian, on their behalf.

Murray Cochrane
Hazel Brasington (née Cochrane)

Map of India, Bangladesh and Nepal

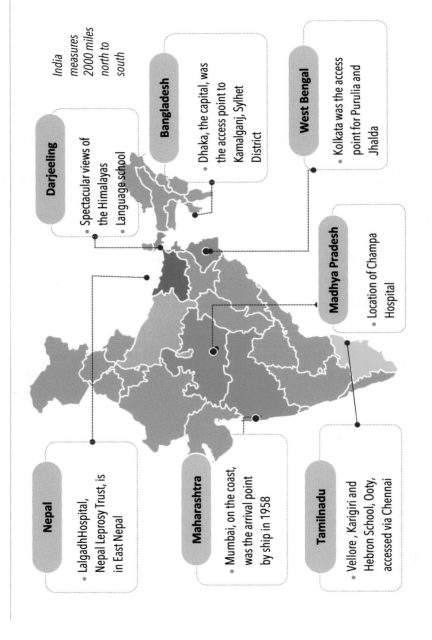

India measures 2000 miles north to south

Darjeeling
- Spectacular views of the Himalayas
  Language school

Bangladesh
- Dhaka, the capital, was the access point to Kamalganj, Sylhet District

West Bengal
- Kolkata was the access point for Purulia and Jhalda

Madhya Pradesh
- Location of Champa Hospital

Nepal
- LalgadhHospital, Nepal Leprosy Trust, is in East Nepal

Maharashtra
- Mumbai, on the coast, was the arrival point by ship in 1958

Tamilnadu
- Vellore, Karigiri and Hebron School, Ooty, accessed via Chennai

Key Dates

Event	Date
Marion Grace Tuckwell born in Southampton	April 1928
Children's nurse training and nursing roles, Southampton Children's Hospital	1946-1950
General nurse training and nursing roles, St, Mary's Hospital, London	1951-1954
Nursing in Toronto, Canada, Midwifery training in Kent, Nursing in Brighton	1954-1958
Ian and Marion married in Southampton	May 1958
Ian and Marion sail to India	October 1958
Leprosy Mission Hospital, Purulia, West Bengal, including Darjeeling for language training	1958-1965
Leprosy Mission, Jhalda, West Bengal	1965-1970
Leprosy Mission Hospital, Champa, Madhya Pradesh including Salur, Andhra Pradesh for surgical training	1970-1977
Back to Purulia, with visits elsewhere including Karigiri	1978-1979
Health, Education and Economic Development project, Kamalganj, Sylhet District, Bangladesh	1980-1990
Leprosy Co-ordinating Committee, Dhaka, Bangladesh	1990-1993
Anandaban, Nepal	1993
Investiture of MBE by Her Majesty the Queen	1993
Nepal Leprosy Trust, Lalgadh Hospital, Nepal	1993-1996
Ian and Marion return to the UK	1996

CHAPTER ONE

How it all began

As a young nurse in London I regularly attended meetings run by the Nurses' Christian Fellowship. We had a series of interesting speakers who valiantly came late in the evening after we finished duty. One left an indelible impression, showing us a film about people with leprosy in India. I was shocked to see the devastating injuries and not realising that they were largely painless felt a revulsion and horror. I said to myself, "I could NEVER do that work". As a Christian I would help by giving money and praying, but nothing more.

With the prospect of nursing in Canada, this event was put to the back of my mind. Training and further experience in the hospital was over and I was looking for fresh fields to conquer in my professional progress. My new St. Mary's 'Penny' brooch – awarded after qualifying from St. Mary's Hospital, Paddington - had my name inscribed on the back as well as the motto in Latin which comes from the book of Ecclesiastes chapter 9 verse 10, '*Whatever your hand finds to do, do it with your might.*'

A friend and I applied to work in the famous Hospital for Sick Children in Toronto. Our training certificates and credentials safely in our luggage, we enjoyed the Atlantic crossing in 1956 on the *Franconia*. For me, there was the added excitement of exploring Canada because my Father had previously emigrated there in 1913, only to return at the start of World War 1 when he volunteered to join the Merchant Navy. He then stayed with the Merchant Navy until he retired.

Learning the ways of a different country proved a steep learning curve, with a different currency and terminology, even though English was spoken. When we found accommodation and took the tramcar to reach the hospital,

I gave a note to the driver and receiving, as I thought, the change, I moved down the car to be hailed by loud protests for failing to pay my fare. I had been given the full exchange in coins rather than change -a lesson learnt the hard way! We soon learnt the value of the strange coins and the different methods.

A year of work there gave opportunities to travel as we made the most of days off, attached to the statutory holidays. The Canadian main cities, Niagara Falls, plus New York, Philadelphia, Washington were all ticked off as we made good use of Greyhound coaches for economical travel, often overnight. Our main holiday saw us on the train across to the west coast, stopping off to see cities on the four-day journey. So, to Vancouver and then over to Vancouver Island by ferry. Each city held its own appeal, adding fresh interest to the trip and the picturesque island was no exception.

Once more the Atlantic crossing was enjoyed on the return to the UK in 1957, this time sailing from New York on my father's old ship the *Queen Elizabeth*, on which he had been an electrical engineer. Word soon travelled that 'Tucky's daughter' was on board and, along with other nurses on the ship, we received some VIP hospitality including a visit to the engine rooms.

Finding a job back in the old country became the next priority. There seemed to be two options, one in Brighton and one much further north. Brighton by the sea sounded much more attractive and nearer my parents in Southampton. There I returned to the blue uniform, black stockings and stiff cuffs, taking up my position as Sister on the children's ward.

Soon a young child was admitted with a fracture which needed the application of what was known as the gallows, so the legs were upright with the body at right angles on the bed. I was back doing things that in Canada only the doctors had done. The casualty doctor, Ian Cochrane, came daily to check on the young child's condition in this static position. Later, after completing the notes, he mentioned tennis, as there was a tennis court behind the hospital. We arranged to play, but he did not mention he had not really played before, only purchasing a racquet and balls to use for the occasion. He asked me to keep the score. Playing my best tennis, I won. Ian said, "We'll have to have another game, sister!" I never won again on repeated games.

Life continued and with his six months over he moved up to Birmingham for his next rotation at Selly Oak Hospital. However, there was the suggestion we meet again when he returned to visit family in the area. We had much in common with our respective plans, mine to go to Africa and his to go to India to do medical work with leprosy. His going within the year and mine much delayed by years of further training, required by the Christian mission. Several months later, after meeting only 2-3 times, due to my alternate weekends off and his every third weekend, we met the weekend before Christmas at my parents' home, where I had taken gifts, due to working over the holiday period. To everyone's surprise, not least mine, he 'popped the question' and I said "YES!" The wedding was planned after his parents' return from Africa, where his father was doing leprosy consultancy and training courses.

In those days we had to obtain permission to marry from his sending mission, not like his father who had to work for four years with a long engagement, then take his bride out! Blissfully unaware I was being vetted, I enjoyed invitations to splendid teas with older doctors and their wives. I must have passed the test, for our marriage was approved. We knew that without approval we would have to go our separate ways. Plans were made for us to travel to India by ship in October 1958; he returning to his childhood home and taking a completely 'green' wife, as far as Asia was concerned.

Before we left, a visit was arranged to one of the two leprosy hospitals in the UK at that time, in Redhill (the other one was in Chelmsford). The visit was relished by Ian and dreaded by me. We duly arrived and soon the charming doctor in charge took us to see patients. I was being thrown in at the deep end as I was asked to feel an enlarged nerve at a man's elbow. My arm froze. Only an arrow prayer "Dear Lord, I have to TOUCH this man" saved the day as I remembered reading in the bible 'Unclean DON'T TOUCH' (Leviticus chapter 13). My belief in the power of prayer rocketed sky high that day. After what seemed a long time to me, but probably only a few seconds, I felt the large nerve and any fear of leprosy vanished immediately. Here I had my first encounter with leprosy patients and could put behind me those unfounded fears instilled by that film some years earlier. I only hope my inner fear was not visible on my face to that

3

man, but I have to thank him for introducing me to some of the most wonderful and courageous people I have had the privilege of meeting since. A lesson learnt about use of the word NEVER. Be careful how you use it for what you feel you could never do may well be the very thing God calls you to do. For if He calls you, HE will enable you to do it - as I have proved!

St. Mary's 'Penny' awarded on qualification

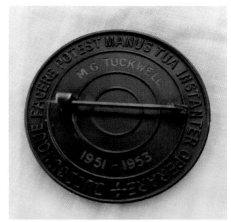

Motto and inscription on St. Mary's Penny

On the *Franconia* en route to Canada, 1956

Returning to the UK on the *Queen Elizabeth* with nursing friends, 1957

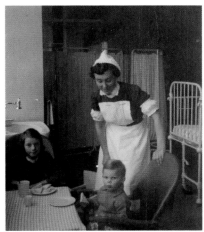

'Sister Tuckwell', Brighton 1956

Our wedding day, 17 May 1958

CHAPTER TWO

Sailing to India

1958 was a very eventful year, starting with a refresher course in midwifery, with a view to completing part 2, as prescribed by the Baptist Missionary Society to which I had offered my services.

However, meeting Ian changed all that, and instead I was busy planning our wedding, after the 6-weeks' course.

We were married on 17 May at Shirley Baptist Church, Southampton, before moving to Beckenham in South London, so Ian could commute to St. Bartholomew's Hospital (Barts) outpatient department. I, meanwhile, worked in the outpatient department at Beckenham Hospital and started packing for India. The upstairs flat gradually filled with boxes and trunks ready for India.

We sailed in October, complete with 24 packages, which included 3 tea chests of books (well half books and topped up with cushions and other light items, so they could be handled), two bicycles, a kerosine refrigerator, a piano accordion and tape recorder plus personal items and clothes.

We sailed from Southampton on the *Chusan* – a second honeymoon - and arrived in Bombay two weeks later, briefly visiting Ian's sister, Margaret, in Aden en route. Sadly, there was no mention of Peter, whom she married soon afterwards.

Bombay was a huge shock to my western eyes, seeing thin porters/ sahayaks carting loads I had only seen being handled by machines before, but this was India! For Ian it was returning to familiar scenes, but for me it was a huge shock.

Customs was another shock. We were allocated to a certain person, and he was a very difficult man, whom I suspect was not in favour of Christian foreigners. His queue remained long, but other officials had dealt with their clients and left. I do remember thinking, after completing the forms seven times, "This was NOT the welcome I expected. I feel like getting back on the ship…". The patient agent we had was finally able to deal with our baggage and send us to Wilson College, where we were to stay with friends of Leprosy Mission colleagues from India, who had travelled on the ship with us.

The next day our goods were finally cleared through customs and taken to storage prior to us catching the train for a journey of 1,700 kilometres across India to Chakradharpur, which is just short of Calcutta (345 kilometres from Calcutta) – another new experience for me, sharing the room with 2 strange men!

We were delighted and surprised to be met there by the hospital superintendent, who was determined we should be met, unlike his family's arrival. After a curry - which the men enjoyed and I struggled with, even after adding a couple of bananas - we joined the train to Purulia in West Bengal, a couple of hours away.

It was very exciting to arrive there and when we entered the house, I thought we were going into a church hall, complete with pillars, and said so to Ian, who smiled benevolently, being familiar with lofty houses (12 feet high walls and top windows). I learned to appreciate them in the hot weather.

It was a relief when a trail of cycle rickshaws arrived the next day with all our boxes (just as the agent had assured me).

I soon started unpacking and was amazed to get dizzy after a while, until reassured by Ian that this was the tropics and I could not expect to keep up the same pace as in the cool west!

White ants were a real menace so bricks under trunks were essential - and constant vigil. When a friend went to pack her case to leave, she only lifted the handle, for white ants had devoured the case!

Apart from a tour of the hospital we were in the house unpacking and starting Bengali lessons daily. Our teacher came early before school, arriving on his sit up and beg cycle with flowing dhoti – a white cloth wrapped around the waist. It took me a month to learn the alphabet and write it.

By the time Christmas came we had a few words of Bengali but were not able to follow all the high Bengali words used in worship. I did not realise we needed to learn two languages really, the village Bengali - as spoken locally *and* the high language of literature. 'Amen' is the same, fortunately!

The child patients came carol singing and we gave them each an orange. I had helped prepare the gifts for child patients: a cloth bag containing a comb, soap, flannel and another small item.

Christmas was celebrated with many services, and a special 'Love feast' served by the staff. This included meat (mutton) and a large portion of rice and dhal (lentils), and vegetable curry, all served on banana leaves. Moslem cooks were employed specially to butcher the meat and cook this feast. In those days there were several hundred patients, so it was quite an undertaking. It amazed me how much rice one person could eat.

Ian enjoyed playing carom (an Indian game that involves flicking pieces into nets in each corner of the board) with the healthy girls who lived in a hostel next to our house. It also helped his Bengali.

After three weeks one of our friends from the U.K moved away to Kodam Tolla (the house under the shade of the Kodam trees.) So, I had to struggle with Bengali on my own and try and talk to the two staff members - a cook and cleaner. I found having staff in the house a new and daunting experience, but quickly realised they were essential in that climate. It was my first experience of house staff, so essential in the heat and dust with the need to boil drinking water and milk daily.

So, a memorable year came to an end. My first of many in the east.

CHAPTER THREE

Life in India

Darjeeling for language training

Once in India, we needed to go to language school to learn Bengali. This was held for three months up in Darjeeling.

The train journey from Calcutta was broken by a river crossing, where porters/sahayaks carried our luggage, and we went through the sandy banks to join the Darjeeling Mountain Railway on the other side. The hill train then chugged up the mountain at a steady pace until we arrived in Darjeeling, at an altitude of about 7000 feet, thankful for warm clothes and the end of travel.

Language study and pregnancy are not happy memories; the cottage where we stayed had a wonderful view of snow peaked mountains and the valley below. But mould soon grew on all our clothes and it WAS cold!

There, on a daily basis, clouds permitting, we had glorious views of the Himalayas. The Kanchenjunga range with its snow-clad peaks were a joy to behold when the sun shone and the mist cleared. The cold mountain air should have cleared my brain to retain the teaching but sadly it was not so, as I struggled to remember all these strange sounds and words. Perhaps the damp, cold accommodation had something to do with it. I have never before or since seen mould grow on clothes hanging in the wardrobe!

Later in the year I travelled alone to Vellore in south India ready for my son Murray's arrival, flying from Calcutta to Madras (Chennai). My kind hosts for that period were Dr H and Mrs Z Gass. Herb worked with Robert Cochrane in leprosy.

Two years later we were again in Darjeeling. Most folk go two years running but we had been down in Vellore and Karigiri, South India to absorb more knowledge about leprosy. This time we were in a different house with a toddler, which was less damp, but I do remember the acute water shortage. When it rained, I put out teacups to catch the drops from each corrugation of the roof so I had water to wash the nappies!

Visiting Calcutta (Kolkata)

Our first trip to Calcutta was for shopping. Yards of mosquito netting to make a net for our 7' bed, which was made of two single beds together. 'Dalda' in a very large tin - like a kerosine tin and containing something similar to margarine. This was before the 'piriwalla' caught on to the large trade for expats in Purulia.

We stayed at the Baptist Missionary Society guest house and I remember being awakened by the many crows squawking in the early morning in the large tree outside. We certainly gave the porters/sahayaks income to transport all these items to the train at Howrah station, where we arrived in two taxis. After our son, Murray was born, we went to Carey Baptist Church in Calcutta for his dedication, along with proud Granny Cochrane. We stayed at the house of the minister, after his wife had been to Purulia for a break.

For Hazel's birth, I made an extra trip back to the UK. Two years after Murray's dedication, we again went to Calcutta for Hazel's dedication.

I remember standing in the small pulpit from which William Carey preached, feeling duly honoured and humbled. We also visited Serrampore College, to see a couple from language school who were working there. It is awe-inspiring to think of working in the same area as the founder of the Baptist Missionary Society.

South India

We could see some hills from Vellore Hospital and the college compound was beside what we called College Hill. It was one of several in the area and in the cool of the evening we could clamber up one of them for a better scenic view and to get some fresh air and exercise following days working in Dermatology outpatients for Ian and in leprosy physiotherapy for me.

We later moved to Karigiri, where the Leprosy Research Hospital was situated. My father-in-law had helped to select the site and had divined water there, although it was rather barren by the hill. The name 'Karigiri' means elephant hill, for it was shaped like the back of an elephant. We climbed this many times in the evenings and I have a picture of us with a Vellore-made backpack with holes in for our son's legs. I think of this when I see the beautifully purpose-made ones now available for my great grandson!

Several years later we would drive with my father-in-law to Vadathorasalur through these hills, one of which was called Moses. This was the day when my mother-in-law had been buried at the Vellore cemetery. He had finally retired from all the globe-trotting activities and they were looking forward to two years together in Vadathorasalur. But God had other plans and after only six weeks there she died.

Vellore came to a halt as the huge procession from the hospital to the cemetery included busloads of students, many doctor colleagues and patients supporting their previous Director and Principal in his great grief. We were thankful to the Leprosy Mission India Director for allowing us to travel south (with literally half an hour's notice) to make the journey by train. I thought I would be nursing her after a stroke, but we arrived just in time for the funeral. This was before the days of mobile 'phones and e mails.

Mountains are hard to scale, and this goes for the mountains we experience in life. The hardships and problems are temporary but the promise of God's presence and help through it all means we shall overcome and be victorious in His strength.

Furlough

We attempted to make ice-cream when the children were young. It was a task which involved almost frozen ice cubes and flavoured milk. A less happy episode was when Ian was tempted to eat ice cream in Calcutta during the saga to complete paperwork so we could leave the country for a trip home on furlough. I was travelling south by train to collect the children from boarding school. We all met up in Poona (Pune) to spend a couple of days with a friend before joining the ship in Bombay (Mumbai). Meeting Ian off the train he announced he thought he had flu. However, it was much worse, revealed by a blood test, for he had enteric fever. The Scottish lady doctor caring for him, declared that he would not be able to travel unless the high, debilitating fever came down, for without support he could not get from bed to the adjoining bathroom. How we prayed, and thankfully the fever subsided. Strange, I thought, it was always the fear of children with chicken pox or similar, which might prevent our travel. We made it to the ship, the *Chitral*, and as the Suez Canal was closed, we had a month going around Africa - a wonderful convalescence with rest, sea air and good food, not to mention the much-appreciated time as a family. So again, what seemed to be a possible disaster became a beneficial chapter in our lives.

Jhalda, West Bengal

After seven years interrupted by language school, the arrival of two children and home leave, we were asked to move out of Purulia. Leprosy work was changing with the advent of drugs to cure it, meaning long stays in the hospital and a 'home for life' were no longer required. We were to be part of this changing emphasis. Our headquarters would be in Jhalda, 30 miles from Purulia. Here we could establish the new model and the many satellite clinics held monthly, keeping patients in their homes and villages, without the need of rehabilitation. The clinic was already functioning with numbers increasing, just as they had in the outpatients department in Purulia, creating the need for more clinics.

I was anchored at the clinic compound while Ian spent most of his time setting up and visiting clinics in various villages where leprosy patients were plentiful. Initially we occupied a room in the clinic, while a doctor's house was being constructed. Pressure was on for its rapid completion so we could have the children home from boarding school and my parents (visiting from the U.K.) plus Ian's father, now a widower, for Christmas. We moved in while porters/sahayaks still walked through carrying eight bricks on their heads to complete the upstairs bedroom for the children. Sadly, while doing this, my engagement ring was stolen from the clothes drawer. We did battle with heavy, ill-fitting metal doors, deemed important for security in this village setting.

We inherited a dog called Caesar, to which we added the name Disgustus, as I frequently had to give money to some villager who presented me with a skinny dead chicken he was said to have killed. The school holidays came and went. It was only when I packed the trunks for them to return to boarding school in January that the losses of underwear were discovered. I am sure the Marks and Spencer underwear was valued and hopefully survived the thrashing on stones when washed! I realised more must be bought locally to fulfil the boarding school kit list. These were not as durable as the ones bought in the UK.

Soon there were monthly clinics established in over 20 villages from where many patients came. This meant that most days the clinic jeep travelled with staff, records and medicines, helping to ensure regular treatment, so vital and often not possible due to poverty and lack of transport. Patients were encouraged to take regular treatment, nearer home, taking their 'blister packs' with a month's tablets.

Meanwhile I held health education classes for staff wives and others using a growing stock of flannelgraphs. Pictures were used to teach those remaining at home about the importance of regular treatment, general health etc. The high degree of illiteracy made the picture form very important. A flannelgraph set for Bible stories was used and adapted for health education which was much needed. Skills with a puppet were also put to use and much appreciated. Hopefully this aided the memory to put into practice what was taught about hygiene, diet and diseases.

The barren hill was soon planted with trees and bushes (too many it seems years later). We planted a garden and enjoyed clean water from the well. The tank used for soaking bricks became a small swimming pool, much appreciated in the hot summer months and secluded by bougainvillea.

Foot ulcers are a big problem for leprosy patients, for they lack feeling and therefore feel no pain, as we would. They keep walking when we would keep a painful foot up and resting. This is where a Plaster of Paris comes in very useful. The patient can walk and rest the ulcer at the same time, so promoting healing. Even this is not fool proof, as we discovered with one teenage boy. He seemed unable to keep the Plaster of Paris dry and intact. They were repeatedly applied and re-applied until finally, to our relief, the ulcer under his foot healed. But how to keep him ulcer free? The solution was to provide him with a cycle rickshaw. He was delighted to earn money ferrying passengers around the village, and we were delighted that as well as a healed ulcer he had some form of earning money to keep him usefully active and hopefully ulcer free.

The villagers were very poor and one day a malnourished child with a huge pot belly was brought to the clinic. Clearly, she needed protein which was beyond the mother's purse. As well as teaching to give less rice with a little lentils, she was given a few crushed peanuts and dried milk each day. What a joy to see her come to life, smile and look more normal as weeks went by.

After five years, Jhalda was well established with capable national staff and we moved on again.

Champa

My good friend and colleague, Mollie Clarke and I decided we were going to be permanently in West Bengal while other staff were moved on. How wrong we were! She was then asked to go to Bhutan and us to Champa in Madhya Pradesh. Her book, '*Mountains, medicine and miracles*' on the 17 years in Bhutan is fascinating reading.

The advent of multi-drug therapy (MDT) soon brought the leprosy problem under control and many clinics were later closed down. My book about Dr R G Cochrane, '*The edge of the cliff*' gives background to treatment advances in recent years too.

It was only latterly that I understood the years of clinic work were not really enjoyed by Ian, so the move to the hospital in Champa was very welcome. There may have been lack of enjoyment, but it was a very productive period.

Many years later when back in the UK after retirement I was asked to support the Champa night watchman, when he was invited to Bournemouth to receive the Wellesley Bailey award. Created in 1999 to celebrate the life and work of Mr Wellesley Bailey, founder of The Leprosy Mission, these awards are a unique and prestigious honour. Each recipient has made extraordinary contributions to society through overcoming the social stigma and physical challenges of leprosy. What a wonderful surprise for both of us! I recall many disturbed nights in Champa due to the incessant banging of the night watchman's stick on his rounds!

Kanchenjunga (8,586 metres) forms the backdrop to The Darjeeling Himalayan Railway in a gift of this picture from a UK doctor on their elective.

Our Bengali language teacher in Darjeeling (centre), with her family

Setting off by train from Lushington Hall in the Nilgiri hills – Murray's future school - after one term as the school nurse and a hill holiday in Kotagiri. Ian was at the Vellore Dermatology department. Note the bedding rolls, piano accordion, nappy basket, the cabin trunk from Marion's father's days in the Merchant Navy and the small brown case which contained the library!

View of the hospital at Christian Medical College, Vellore, founded by Dr Ida Scudder. Murray was born here at 4am on 24 October 1959 (still 23 October in the UK!)

'Big Bungalow', Christian Medical College, Vellore. A previous residence of Robert and Ivy Cochrane

College Hill, Vellore, 1961. Ian carrying Murray in a rucksack made for the purpose

A family send-off after a trip to the UK for Hazel's birth in 1961.

International Leprosy Congress Gala Dinner, London, 1963. Ian wearing a tie given by David Bowen on the the *Chusan* at Bombay in 1958. Marion wearing a Chinese silk dress, made up in Calcutta by Joan Staunton's tailor with cloth given by my mother-in-law, Ivy Cochrane

Aden in 1963, en route between India and the UK, with a chance to see Ian's sister Margaret. Our ship, the *Chusan*, is in the background.

With Ian's sister, Margaret, on a boat in Aden.

The hill train at Coonoor in the Nilgiri hills, South India, where Hazel later went to school. We were en route for Ooty, for Murray to go to school in May 1965. The Nilgiri Mountain Railway was built in 1908 and declared a UNESCO World Heritage site in 2005.

CHAPTER FIVE

Leprosy work in Bangladesh

I have been reading a book called, 'You will meet Hoopoes'. We certainly saw them in Bangladesh. They are so dramatic in flight, with their black and white striped wings and black tips to the large crests atop their heads.

I well remember after a particularly hard day in the hospital, walking up through the trees to our house, which was built a discreet distance from the Leprosy hospital. Suddenly a beautiful golden oriel dipped across in front of me! It was such a lovely sight and restored my equilibrium and my sanity!

Blue Jays were also a familiar sight which I miss now back in the U.K., their bright blue colour flashing in the sun.

On business trips to Dhaka for the Leprosy Co ordinating Committee, I always got back into the train for the six-hour journey thankful we were not called to work in noisy, congested, polluted cities. For most leprosy hospitals are in quieter, remote places, even outside villages. This meant residents were not exposed to the supposed dangers of being near other patients. We had the needed drugs for treatment to cure the disease, and Ian did some reconstructive surgery to deformed hands and feet - sadly the result of delayed treatment due to fear or neglect.

The most wonderful part of being in the team at the leprosy hospital was being able to show the patients that we cared for, and accepted them, and could show them a better way of life by caring for their unfeeling hands and feet. Adapting tools and working methods gave back some self-esteem. This enabled not only acceptance but a contribution to society. The fact that we were not afraid to touch them also made a big impression. Some patients stand out in the memory as persistent failures and some as a great success. The first group for the need to persist and the second for encouragement.

The need for training more paramedic workers to assist in finding and treating patients in their homes as well as running the many new clinics was addressed when I was asked to run a course for them. I was given just three weeks to prepare. I praise God for the help given by The Leprosy Mission and the tried and trusted materials. All the students passed their exams and the newly appointed doctor also learnt the basics of leprosy and the importance of teamwork. These young men went on to do sterling work in the area and the one female to work in some clinics with the ladies and also in the laboratory.

I remember talking with one of our volunteer physiotherapists from the U.K. We were so pleased she could come to Bangladesh through Voluntary Service Overseas (VSO). She explained that Bangladesh was classified as a 'hardship posting' and so she could only stay for two years. She then asked me how long we had been in Bangladesh. "Oh," I replied, "nearly thirteen years!"

When my niece visited us in Bangladesh, she was very accommodating, as we carried on with our work and she joined in.

World Leprosy Day had come and gone with much preparation and publicity, thanks largely to a grant from the British High Commissioner's discretionary fund. As the co-ordinator, I needed to take an account of how we spent all the money – to them, it was a small grant, but to us the total cost of T shirts, posters and other expenses, which were all covered. The Leprosy Mission was newly registered, and as we had no vehicle of our own, a cycle rickshaw provided transport.

So, we arrived to hand in the financial report. I wore a long dress which had been passed on to me and was made of six square scarves. Only recently, have I discovered the significance of this garment. The prayer guide for Ramadan Day Two, provided the interesting answer. Women in the Comoros Islands wear the traditional Shiromani made from six square scarves. Red always predominates. It is the symbol of the Anjouani culture. I can only hope that my wearing it did not offend the ladies of the Anjouani tribe on the Comoros Islands. I also wore it with pride, in a society where ladies cover up. It was with a heart full of praise (like in Isaiah chapter 61 verse 3), that I went to render the account that day. Our need to proclaim leprosy as curable and that treatment is available had been fulfilled in many ways.

After 13 years in Bangladesh, it was time to move on again, leaving the work in capable national hands. The farewell ceremony was quite something and the fibre optic lamp is still part of the Christmas decorations!

CHAPTER SIX

After a splendid farewell in Bangladesh, we spent some time looking for a house in the UK. We were an estate agent's nightmare. To all his questions we gave the same answer "we don't know". Fortunately, the Lord had it in his capable hands! When looking at a tiny residence with hardly any garden, Ian spotted a board at the end of the Close. 23 Armada Close was to be home for 10 years. It had a garden and a field behind it.

We had hardly unpacked and settled in when we had a request to go to Nepal for two months to relieve a doctor for full time language study. So, we packed our bags and went, thankful for an opportunity to work again; thus, underlining my statement that there is no retirement in the Lord's service.

The hills (mountains in my terminology) were steep and literally took our breath away. I soon found a niche in records, which needed updating. Whilst there we met Eileen Lodge, who enquired if Ian could give her new hospital a kick start! Only out for a short term, he felt unable to go and see it, so I went, taking a whole day to get there. We both knew this was for us but said the final decision would be made in the U.K.

So, once more we set off to a new assignment. Three faithful workers were already seeing leprosy patients as outpatients. The hospital was a building site, with lorries constantly bringing in building supplies and clouds of dust. We lived in the thatched cottage Eileen had occupied.

As soon as possible, one ward for in-patients was established and the work steadily grew. Word of mouth soon proclaimed it was a good place to go. I found plenty to do, ordering supplies, getting uniforms for staff etc., designing forms, the tasks were endless, setting up a hospital.

Eileen had realised that so many patients came from this area when she worked in Pokhara and a more local hospital would mean more regular treatment, rather than two days of travel.

The work has grown tremendously over the years as patients travel long distances to attend. One factor is that patients feel they get value for money rather than bribes, so much part of life, sadly. Overcoming the stigma of leprosy is another factor, and it is a great encouragement that over 80% of the outpatients attending Lalgadh Hospital are non-leprosy patients. This shows that leprosy treatment is increasingly integrated into health care and not kept outside.

Taking the motorbike on a ferry with two paramedics to get to an outlying clinic in Bangladesh.

Ian and Marion at Lalgadh Hospital, south east Nepal, December 1994 – working while the hospital was still under construction at the time.

At Buckingham Palace in 1993 for both Ian and Marion to receive the award of Member of the Order of the British Empire from Her Majesty the Queen.

CHAPTER SEVEN

Looking back

Earliest memories – Bramston Road, Southampton

One of my earliest memories was of a GP visiting the house after my brother, 'playing milkman', had an accident when glass milk bottles broke and he cut his leg, requiring sutures. The GP arrived and I was given strict instructions not to enter the front bedroom. I thought I was obeying this instruction, laying on my tummy with all but my feet in the bedroom, saying "I aren't in", not wanting to miss anything, like most two year olds.

At that time, the milkman collected empty glass bottles when delivering milk and the milk cart was horse-drawn. Later, as a young nurse, I tried to keep in the wheel marks left by the milkman's horse and cart, when cycling to the children's hospital at 7am in the snow. I know the keen gardeners were quick to gather the horse manure for their gardens!

Originally the house had a pebble drive – which my father used when arriving back in the middle of the night from the ship - he threw them at the upstairs window to be let in!

When my father sailed into Southampton on the newly completed *Queen Mary* in 1936, I was there watching with hundreds of others as she sailed into port. Families of the crew were then allowed on board, so on we went to see the ship and my father. He had thoughtfully obtained a block of ice-cream to celebrate this great day, and proudly produced it in his cabin. The only problem was that we had nothing to eat it with, so I grabbed his toothbrush. Lack of cutlery was not going to see me miss out on this latest treat.

World War 2

I dreaded moonlit nights when enemy aircraft flew overhead. The drone of their engines, as they flew, heavy with bombs. We wondered where they were planning to unload them, Coventry? or some other industrial town vital to the war effort? Then we would cheer if we heard spitfires chasing them!

The Morrison table shelter filled the dining room. Its metal top was ideal for table tennis, as long as the wire mesh sides were out of the way. Later we used the Anderson shelter in the back garden of No 15. Only 70 years later was I able to drink cocoa, after the vivid memory of a drink from mother's thermos. The something solid turned out to be an earth worm that had fallen into my cup! Memories of broken biscuits from the tin were more favourable. Deck chairs still hold memories for me, which we kept in the shelter.

About 3 am we would return to our beds after the returning planes heralded the all clear siren. This single note was so welcome after the wailing siren that sent us underground.

There were few 'phones then and so I went with my mother to an old lady's house at the end of Lascelles Road, where my mother had booked a call. The excitement when the phone rang was considerable. We were actually able to speak to my father in Scotland. Being on one of the 'Queens' (*Queen Mary* or *Queen Elizabeth*), the ships only stayed briefly in port - or anywhere - as their size was an enviable target for any Nazi bomber. A train journey would have gobbled up all the time in port and more, so was not always possible. I was excited to hear my father's voice and actually speak to him! When we met two years later, he wondered who was with his wife and then realised it was me, grown much taller than he remembered me.

Most of the time we dreaded 'phone calls, which usually only meant bad news. However, it was a great day when we had a 'phone line much later at 13 Bramston Road and I still remember the number – 73605. How times have changed now with mobiles as well as landlines in most homes.

While at Southampton Grammar School for Girls, Hill Lane (now Richard Taunton Sixth Form College), we had rehearsals for evacuations. I remember two rehearsals before the real evacuation happened. The rehearsal involved bringing in a rucksack to school with a change of clothes and a day's food rations. The day's food rations all got eaten by 10am! When the real evacuation to Bournemouth happened, my mother, my brother and I caught the train and got off at Pokesdown, where we were lucky to stay with Auntie Gracie and Uncle Reg at 19 Lascelles Road. Gracie died of asthma in 1941 and my mother managed the home. Uncle Reg also died in 1942. My mother and brother returned to Southampton before me and I moved to digs with a war widow at 4 Lascelles Road.

Auntie Gracie was my mother's older sister. I had another Auntie - Muriel, who married Uncle Eric and this started many family times together. When Eric and Muriel lived in Shalford near Guildford, my father used to say, "You just need to whisper Shalford under the bonnet and the car knows where to go!"

As well as two Aunts, I also had an Uncle Ernest on my mother's side, who married Gladys from Durban, in South Africa. They had two children – Ethne and Jean, and all of them came over by ship from South Africa. When they arrived at Tilbury Docks, Ernest was taken ill and died. He is buried at the Southampton Cemetery near Southampton General Hospital, along with other relatives on my mother's side. We lost contact with the South African family after this.

An early boyfriend was the second officer on my father's ship, the *Queen Mary*. He had the misfortune to be on the bridge at the time of an accident during World War 2. He had only just come on watch, when a smaller ship crossed the bow of the *Queen Mary* and was spliced in two. My father was in the engine room at the time and felt the shudder. The incident was kept quiet until after the war, as it was important not to give away the ship's location. While living in Axminster, I appreciated my brother, David, letting me know about TV programmes to watch. I had just got back from visiting him while in my 80s when he called to say, "Switch on the TV!". Imagine my surprise to find a programme on the *Queen Mary* and find the screen filled with a picture of my early boyfriend!

Visiting preacher

As a child, I was tasked with talking to the guest while my mother removed the first course remains and produced the pudding, plus freshly made custard, usually some homemade pie or pudding and custard. There was always custard and we children rudely called it the House of Custard.

She often entertained the visiting preacher and so I met one whom I was surprised to meet much later on the stairs of The Leprosy Mission in London, where he was then the editorial secretary.

Then when we were working in Purulia, he came for Christmas and stayed with friends. I remember him talking on Christmas day, probably around 1960.

My last contact was on the Isle of Wight where he and his wife were in a care home.

I still have the St John's Gospel and a picture of Jesus framed in my bedroom, which he gave me, done by a Korean artist. On it there are my photos of those still on active leprosy service around the world.

Nursing in Southampton, Alton, London and Canada

Before being allowed to start nurse training, I had to have my tonsils out – a requirement for all applicants at that time.

At the Southampton Children's Hospital, Winchester Road, I had three years of training in children's nursing and one year as a staff nurse on the ground floor 'D&V' (diarrhoea and vomiting) unit. Working on a hot summer's day as a staff nurse, the babies were all resting after their bed baths and we were writing up their treatment notes when I heard a rather persistent cycle bell ringing. I peered out of the sluice window and there was my mother with two ice-cream cones propped up in her cycle basket. She had purchased them at a nearby sweet shop and pedalled frantically to deliver them before they melted. They were quickly consumed as eating on duty was strictly forbidden. Fortunately for me, the event was not observed by the authorities, so no reprimand was forthcoming.

While posted to Lord Mayor Treloar Hospital in Alton, Hampshire, there was an extremely cold winter in 1947. Even so, tuberculosis patients still had to be outside on the veranda, wrapped in blankets. The stern theatre sister, Joan, said the theatre was dirty and I had to spend all day washing the walls and cleaning. By chance, I came across Joan again around 2010 when I met up with her sister, Mary, who had worked with Robert Cochrane. "Ah, I said, you were the one that made me wash the theatre walls!"

I was advised to train in other branches of nursing in order to progress. St. Mary's Hospital, Paddington, allowed pre-trained nurses to complete general nurse training in two years rather than three.

I remember a tunnel linked the nurses' home and the hospital. In the second year, I met future friends, with whom I would have many adventures. After training, I stayed on as charge nurse in theatres, living at the 'Sisters' home', in a corner building around the gardens and scrubbed for the husband of one nursing friend, who was a surgeon.

A good holiday was spent in Austria with a nursing friend and my cousin. This was more of a sight-seeing holiday with visits to famous castles and a chocolate factory, which we could smell miles before we reached it! The guide told us the employees could eat as much as they liked, for after a week most could not face another single one. So, for chocoholics, you had better go and work in a chocolate factory!

The greatest expedition was our trip to Canada. There is a separate diary of that year long trip. Having obtained a job at the Toronto Hospital for Sick Children, my friend and I travelled on the ship *Franconia* (in 1945 this ship had served as the base for the British delegation in the Black Sea when Churchill, Roosevelt and Stalin met to discuss the shape of post-war Europe) and then by train to stay first at my friend's sister and brother-in-law before moving into the nurses' home. I remember being surprised to see that it took 15 minutes to find a parking spot near the nurses' home. Later, we shared a flat at 102 Spadina Road and after one year, my friend moved to another Canadian city. When she moved away, I moved to a shared flat with five others.

After the year at 'Sick Kids' Toronto, I returned to the U.K. on the *Queen Elizabeth* with several other nurses, sailing from New York. The son of one of my father's friends in New York saw me off with an orchid, instructing me to ask the steward to keep it in a fridge ready for wearing when we arrived in Southampton. News soon travelled to the engine room that 'Tucky's daughter' was on the ship. We were feted at the captain's table and given tours.

I went back to Southampton Children's Hospital and then on to Beckenham to do Part 1 Midwifery training. Whilst at Stone Park Maternity Hospital, Beckenham, I applied to the Baptist Missionary Society who wanted me to complete midwifery training. However, other moves were afoot.

Meeting Ian - 'The rest is history'

When visiting Ian's parents for the first time in Brighton, Ian's father Robert said to me, "So you want to marry my son…. tell me how you make tea." I started my reply "I warm the pot…." He interrupted, "That's enough – you can marry my son!"

Our engagement was announced in the newspaper, in the 'hatch, match and dispatch' section as we called it in our youth. This was followed by the announcement of our wedding - on 17 May 1958. Newspapers were more widely read in those days before the advent of the internet. The Editorial Editor of the Leprosy Mission also put an embarrassing entry in the local paper about a local nurse making good!

Following marriage on 17 May 1958 we moved to Bromley, so commuting to Barts was easy for Ian while I worked at Bromley Hospital.

Before our first trip to India, we went to Keswick with my in-laws. On free afternoons we went boating and my father-in-law, Robert, was happy to row the boat.

We later attended a Keswick-style gathering at Butlins in Filey, going up by coach. After the morning session when Ian, as usual took notes, we were greeted by a man who asked what was to become of all those notes! When we replied, "take them to India" his response was "that is where I was born". So began a long friendship and his home near Heathrow became a regular stop for us going to the airport. I was always happy to be nearer the airport and not risk a missed flight due to delays on the road from Southampton.

Knitting

As a girl, I always remember my Aunt knitting. She made the first suit I had. It was a grey pleated skirt and a matching cardigan with red buttons. I felt the bee's knees when I wore it! So, my love of knitting was born and soon I embarked on my first, a red jumper. It had a complicated pattern of four berries in diamond shaped holes. It made slow progress but was eventually completed and worn with pride, in spite of mother's friend saying I would never finish it! One year, we went on holiday to Cornwall and at low tide, what could a girl do, but sit on the rocks and knit, waiting for the tide to come in again, and go swimming. There is a picture to prove this and underline the comment that I was always knitting, made by a great friend of the family. In the days when we travelled by ship to India, there was plenty of time during the two weeks to play deck games, visit the cinema, swim to get up an appetite for the next meal, and of course, knit. On one voyage all the family learnt to knit. In India we discovered that the boys and men patients knitted, and the girls did sewing and embroidery.

The only knitting I do nowadays is for the Christmas Shoe box appeal. The Christian relief organisation, *Samaritan's Purse*, supply the patterns and gradually through the year there are hats, scarves and hand puppets that double up as gloves. My non-existent artistic skills are evident on the faces of the poor puppets but will doubtless give pleasure to some children as well as help to keep them warm in winter.

Baptist World Assembly – a small world

While nursing in Brighton, my quest for a church led me to Florence Road Baptist Church where the minister who had baptised me at Rosebery Park Baptist Church, Bournemouth during World War 2, was now the minister!

In Brighton, it was also a surprise to find that the organist had stayed with my mother for a month's banking course in Southampton. I had several trips to the beach with his wife and daughter and was also able to get to know her parents.

Many years later, when attending the Baptist Assembly in Bournemouth, I requested to stay with someone from Rosebery Park if possible. It was not only arranged, but my host took me to the church on Sunday morning to meet the same organist's wife after many years, and now a widow. So not only did I enjoy the service but also coffee and a chat with her afterwards.

Another experience was when Ian and I were in Melbourne at the time of the Baptist World Assembly. To our joy there were delegates from Bangladesh and later we enjoyed a meal with them at their host's house, who had also worked there and spoke Bengali.

While in Melbourne, and before the arrival of grandchildren, my daughter and husband had a weekend away. With only public transport available to us, we decided to walk down to Gardiner Uniting Church on Sunday morning. Afterwards, over coffee we mentioned our time in India, which brought the response, "A pity you could not meet Harry Scott-Simmons, who was in India". This prompted our response, "Where is he?!" for Ian and Harry HAD met while in India. Armed with their 'phone number, we arranged to meet briefly, before he and his sister flew to Perth for a family wedding. They lived a stone's throw away. So, while the two ex-Scotch College students chatted, Margaret and I established a friendship which keeps us still in touch and both looking forward to being with the Lord for ever, even though my thought of being a neighbour never materialised.

A chance meeting? No way. All planned I believe. I also had the joy of attending the Dohnavur Fellowship prayer meetings she hosted, when in Melbourne.

I had many times heard my parents speak enthusiastically of Baptist Assemblies and now I was hooked! So, when the Baptist Assembly was in Birmingham I applied for a ticket. Now a widow myself, I was free to go, stayed with friends who were now back from Holland and took the train, like many others.

Imagine my surprise, when joining the vast crowd walking to the venue to see my good friend from Reading and his assistant minister, just ahead of me. I managed to join them but had to leave for the last train before the long programme ended. We were quite a crowd on that train. What a joy to witness all the countries represented in that meeting. In those days we could view the list of attendees.

AFTERWORD

Looking forward - a special invitation

By the way, if someone says to you that the Bible is irrelevant today, you can tell them that I had a re-enactment of the burning bush (Exodus chapter 3) in Axminster. When lightning struck with a loud thunder bolt, a neighbour saw my tree on fire and called the fire brigade. Later that same day, the tree surgeon climbed the tree using his harness to inspect the damage. Once down on the ground again, he announced that there were not even any burnt leaves in the top of the tree. God's power is still active and available to us as His children!

The story of Moses is a familiar one and somehow, I think we feel sorry for Moses when he is told to return to the land from which he had fled! He is now comfortably settled with a wife and family, doubtless trying to forget the murder he committed. Worse still, God tells him to go to Pharaoh. No small wonder that he demurred. God had to use some amazingly powerful signs to convince him that He would be with him, enabling him to fulfil God's plan for His people. Even then, Moses makes excuses that he is slow of speech. Finally, with the promise of Aaron to be the mouthpiece and the promise of God's presence, Moses goes. I wonder if we sometimes prevent great things happening by our lack of faith and fear of the future?

When invitations arrive, they usually come as a pleasant surprise by post. Before we can reply to accept, we check our diaries to make sure we are free that day. Then comes the planning and preparation bit. What present to take and what to wear. Aware of the fact that we have been included in the planned celebration gives us pleasure as well as that of our friends. We wonder who else will be included to share that special day. We feel sorry if we are not able to accept the invitation.

One of my favourite verses in the Bible is Matthew 11 verse 28. It is inscribed on the arch in the church of the Good Samaritan in Purulia, West Bengal in Bengali. People with leprosy find it very welcoming after being shunned by family and friends because of their disease. *"Come to me, all you who labour and are heavy laden, and I will give you rest."* Here is the promise of Jesus and the greatest invitation of all will be when He invites us to join Him for that feast in heaven and to be with Him for ever, away from all the limitations and problems of this earthly life. The closing verses of the Bible in Revelation contain this promise for those who believe in Jesus and trust in Him. I hope to see you there to share the feast!

***

After the death of her husband, Marion continued to be actively engaged with her community, including at The Baptist Church in Kilmington, Devon. She energetically chaired Axminster Churches Together in her 80s; and was a trustee of the Nepal Leprosy Trust until 2019. Marion also took on the demanding project of researching and publishing the book about her father-in-law, Dr Robert Cochrane, '*The edge of the cliff*', another story of a life dedicated to people with leprosy.

Marion wrote the text of the stories in this book and approved the first draft before she died peacefully on 1 January 2022 at the age of 93. She lived a full life dedicated to service. She is much loved, much missed and much admired.

Donations for this book would be gratefully received by The Leprosy Mission and Nepal Leprosy Trust.

Contact details for The Leprosy Mission:

Goldhay Way, Orton Goldhay, Peterborough PE2 5GZ.
Telephone: 01733 370505   www.leprosymission.org.uk

Contact details for the Nepal Leprosy Trust:

10A The Vineyard, Richmond, Surrey, TW10 6AQ.
Telephone: 020 8940 1200   www.nlt.org.uk